Questions That Will Get You (And Others) Talking

DIANE WESTON

Published by Monkey Publishing

Edited by Emily Hutchinson
Design by Jana Rade
Cover Design by Ivica Jandrijevic
Printed by Amazon

1st Edition, published in 2022

Rheinstr. 9
12159 Berlin
Germany

ISBN: 978-3-910282-02-5

Being able to talk about any subject improves relationships both on a personal level and in the workplace.

Intro

Being able to talk about any subject is a valuable skill. It improves relationships both on a personal level and in the workplace. We're not all born with a natural ability to be good conversationalists, but it is a skill you can learn and improve on, quite simply by talking. Thinking of topics to talk about, finding that starting point, can be the hardest part. But that's all made easy with Questions that Will Get You (and Others) Talking. The book that starts your conversations for you!

These questions cover a huge range of topics. Some will make you laugh and some will have you delving into the depths of your brain for the answer. Some may touch on emotional topics, while others will have you questioning your own beliefs. Perhaps you find it hard to open up to others, or maybe you struggle when it comes to asking more personal questions. This book will help you overcome these problems, giving you a doorway to a closer relationship.

How you use this book is up to you, but we encourage you not to rush. The questions within these pages have been specially curated to encourage conversation. You begin with the question, you follow with the answer, and you see where this takes you! Just one question could be the beginning of a whole evening of interesting dialogue. From discovering someone's bad habits, to learning about their greatest fears, the human mind is a fascinating thing to explore.

duction

What are you waiting for?

We do recommend that you work through each section of 10 questions in order as you'll find the questions become more in depth and personal as you work through the section. This makes conversations flow more freely for those who may find it a little difficult to talk about their thoughts and feelings. We start out with the easier questions, and work up to those that may be more emotive. Learning the art of conversation, eloquently answering questions and being able to talk freely about life's difficult topics will truly boost your confidence.

Perhaps you'll work through a section on date night or maybe you'll use the book as an interesting way to pass the time on a long car journey. How ever, you use these conversation starters, the end result will be a greater knowledge of yourself and others, and some interesting times. Friendships and romantic relationships will grow stronger, and you'll gain some great conversational skills that will be of use to you many times in your daily life, across a huge range of situations.

So what are you waiting for? There's a fascinating conversation just waiting for over the page...

What excites you most in the world?

What is the most terrible movie you've ever watched?

If you could travel anywhere in the world this instant, where would it be?

Do you still have any of your childhood toys?

What topic would you talk about at a party where small talk was banned?

What law would you pass first if you were President?

If you could talk to anyone you wanted for an hour, who would it be?

What excites you most in the world?

Do you think there are any similarities between celebrities in the media and the people you know?

What were your first impressions of your partner?

What are your greatest worries?

Which movie do you never get bored of watching?

What is the spiciest food you've ever eaten and did you enjoy it?

What's the best thing that happened today?

If your life was like a TV show, which show would you choose?

What's the best thing that's ever happened to you at work?

Have you changed much since you were a child? In what ways?

What is one thing you'd like to do that would make the world a better place?

Have you ever read a book that changed your life? What was it?

If you had just one month to live, what would you do?

What is your greatest fear?

What's the best thing that's ever happened to you at work?

Who would you least like to be stuck in an elevator with?

If you could change one thing about your school or your job, what would it be?

What's the best type of movie to watch in the theatre?

Have you ever won a prize, and what was it for?

What's your favorite way to relax?

Are you good at choosing gifts for people? What makes it hard or easy?

Do you think social media is a good or bad thing and why?

If you could completely change your appearance, what would you look like?

Which emotion do you find hardest to deal with, and why?

If you could change one thing in your past, what would it be?

4

Diane Weston

What is the best or weirdest themed restaurant you've ever eaten in?

What is the most valuable thing you own?

If you had to change your name, what would you be called?

What smell makes you the happiest?

What would you like to be famous for?

If you could employ someone to help you for an hour every day, what would they do?

If you could change one part of your body, what would it be?

Do you think what people find attractive has changed over the generations?

What inscription would you have on your gravestone?

What's most likely to make you feel better when you're sad?

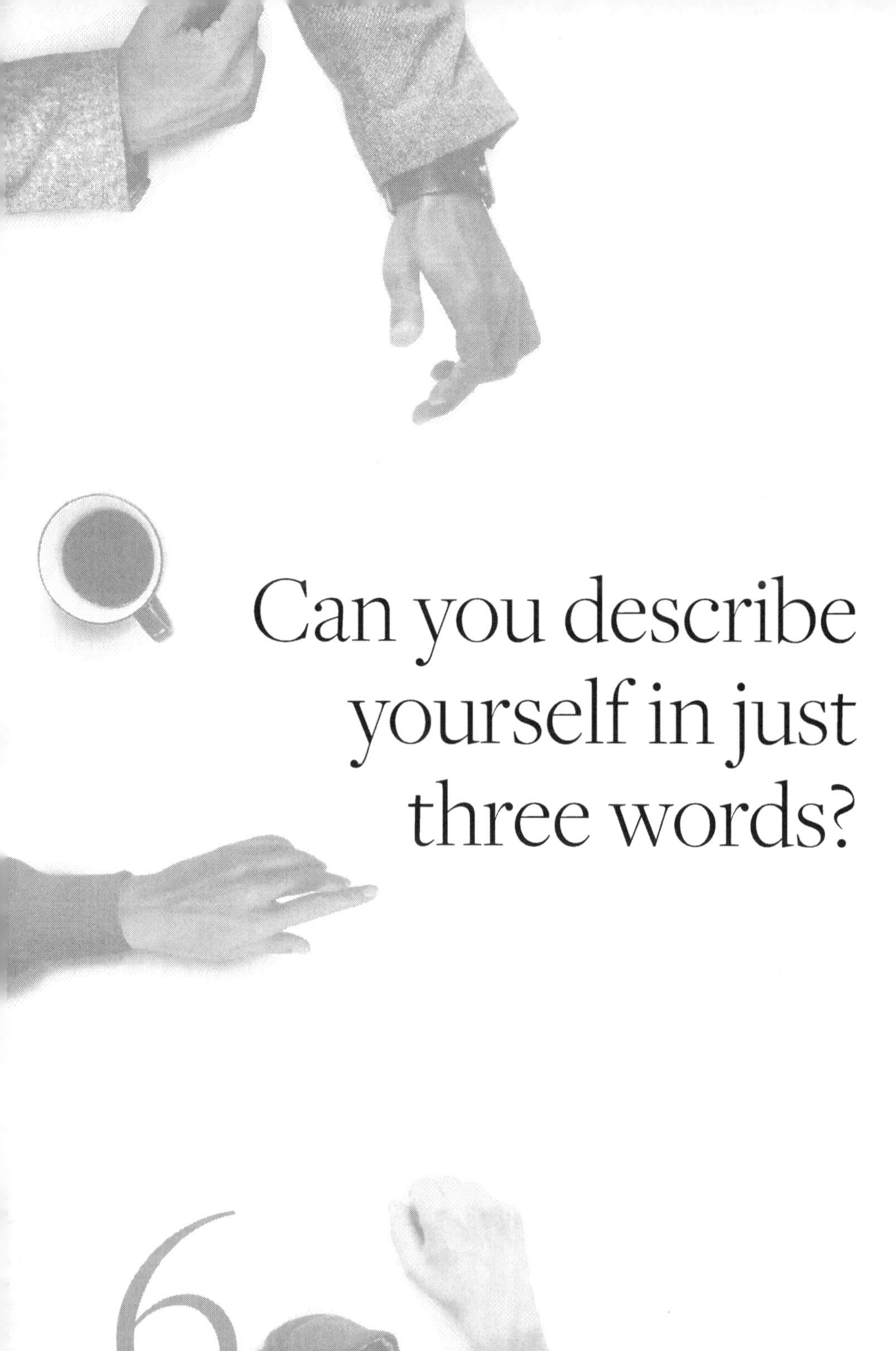

Can you describe yourself in just three words?

6

Diane Weston

What TV shows do you most like to binge watch?

If you could add an extra room to your house, what you use it for?

If you could have anything to eat right now, what would it be?

If you were a superhero, what costume would you wear?

What do people think about you, or your job, that are just not true?

If you could have one question about your future answered, what would you ask?

Is there anything you loved as a child but hate now or vice versa?

Can you describe yourself in just three words?

What's the most embarrassing thing that's ever happened to you?

What have been your biggest challenges in life?

What's your favorite place to go on vacation?

What app do you use the most on your phone?

What's the most fascinating fact you've ever learned?

What's the best gift you've been given?

If your pets could talk, what do you think they'd say to you?

Which celebrities do you think are the most influential?

What's the best way to stay happy in a long-term relationship?

What habits or qualities have you inherited from your parents?

What song is most likely to make you cry?

Do you think you have a purpose in life? If so, what is it?

What sport would you really love to take part in or go and watch?

Who in your family gives the best and worst gifts?

What tech gadget most excited you when you first got it?

What do you dream of doing that you've never done before?

Have you ever watched a film that you really didn't understand? What was it?

In what situations are you most happy to share your opinions?

Do you think your social media posts show an accurate representation of your life?

Is there anything more important to you than good health?

Have you ever broken a rule? What happened?

Who in your life has helped you the most?

What extra body part would you find most useful?

What trends do you think will come back into fashion?

What was the last thing you bought and
are you happy you bought it?

What charities do you most care about?

What social occasions do you most
enjoy and who do you go with?

What romantic gesture would you find most appealing?

What would you do to most express
that you loved someone?

Do you think humankind is mostly
getting things right or wrong?

What was the worst thing about being a kid?

Have you ever experienced love
at first sight? Did it last?

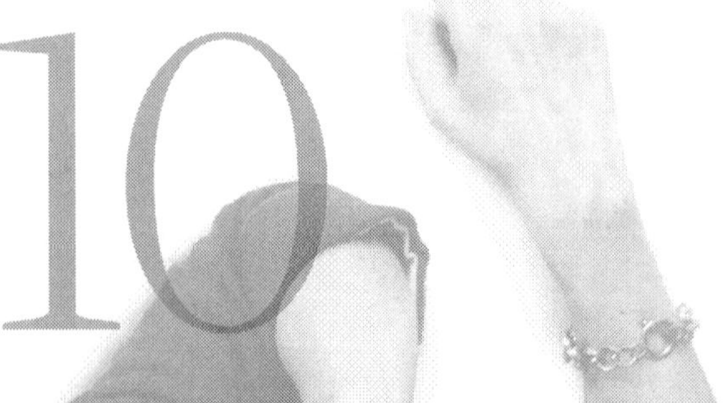

10

Diane Weston

What was the worst thing about being a kid?

What's your ultimate comfort food?

What was your first ever job?

What's your favourite time of day?

Do you have any talents? What are they?

If you could have any job in the world, what would you do?

Have you ever been on a really awful date? What happened?

Are you good at taking tests? Do they make you nervous?

Have you ever been bullied in real life or online?

Have you ever saved a life? How did it happen?

What did you learn as a child that has shaped your life?

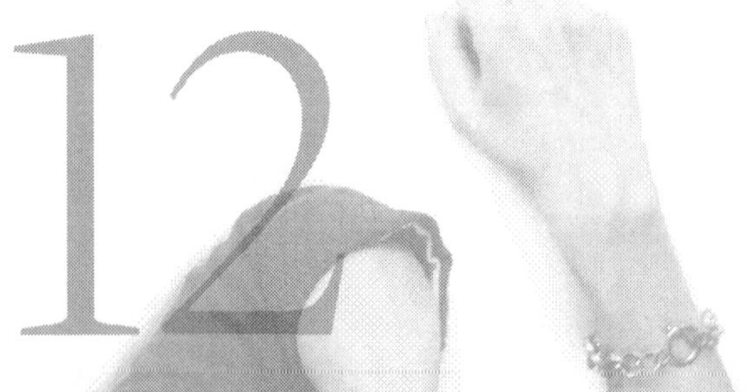

If you were to go on a vacation alone, where would you most like to go?

If you were given a million dollars to spend in a year, how would you spend it?

If you could only recommend one TV series, one movie and one band or singer, what would be your choices?

If you wanted to make a good impression, what meal would you cook someone?

Have you ever been in a situation where you couldn't believe what you were seeing?

Who do you most respect in the world?

What did you want to be when you grew up?

Who do you turn to when you need a shoulder to cry on or someone to talk to?

What is it that makes someone a friend rather than an acquaintance?

Above all, what do you look for in a partner?

What's the best live entertainment you've ever seen?

If you could take up any hobby what would it be?

What things don't you mind spending a lot of money on?

Do you own any plush toys and do you cuddle them?

What's your favorite type of book?

How would you most easily make someone laugh?

What's the worst thing you've experienced or overheard in a restaurant?

If you could change places with anyone in the world, who would it be?

Are you closest to your friends or your family?

What do you wish you were better at?

Have you ever had a food fight? How did it start?

What do you think is the worst ever fashion trend?

What's the best thing that's happened this year?

If you could have one more season of any TV show from the past, what would it be?

What's your favorite thing to do after a busy day at work?

What are the best and worst things about your home town?

What's the best way to throw a really good party?

How do you keep yourself motivated?

What goals have you set yourself and achieved?

If you could break a law and get away with it, what would you do?

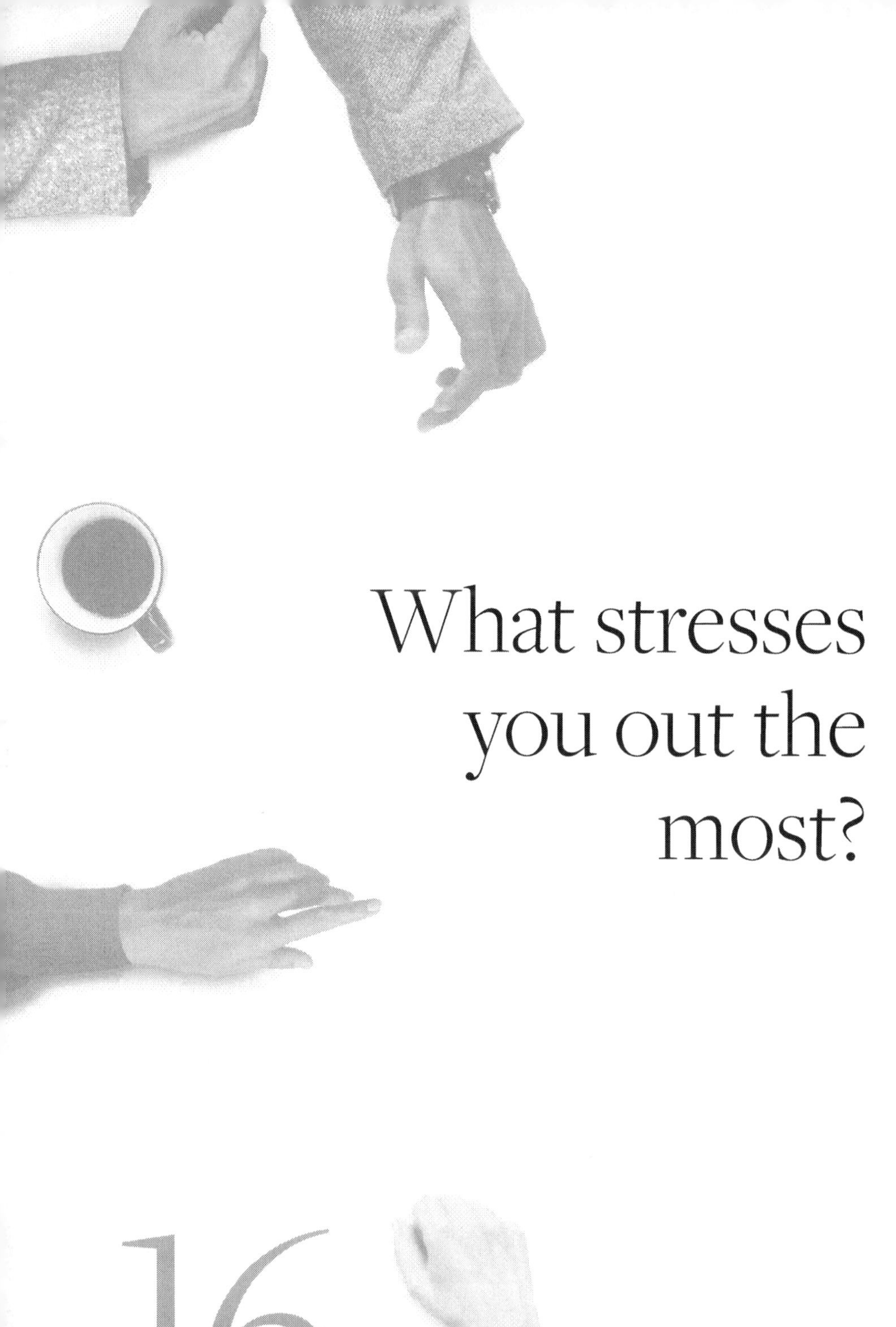

What stresses you out the most?

16

Diane Weston

What's your favorite way to travel?

In your opinion, what is the best genre of music?

What's the best city you've ever visited?

If you had a week off, would you spend it at home or go on vacation?

What's your morning routine?

Do you ever compare yourself with people featured on advertising?

Do you think you're similar to your friends, or very different?

What do you think would be most likely to bring world peace?

What stresses you out the most?

If you're a parent, what could your kids do that would upset you the most? Or, what upset your parents the most when you were a kid?

What type of shop could you spend the most time browsing in?

What would be your dream home and where would it be?

What subject could you talk about for the longest?

What expensive item do you most regret buying?

What foods do you truly hate?

When the zombie apocalypse happens – what's your plan?

What would you change about your current relationship?

What do you do that shows you care about the environment?

If you could improve your health in one way, what would it be?

What would make you end a relationship?

What's the best song for a party playlist?

How well would you cope if you didn't have a cell phone for a week?

What music is best to exercise to?

What movie do you hate that other people love?

What are your first thoughts on waking?

What's more important, a home you love or a life of travel?

If you had the chance of a one-way ticket through a portal to another universe, would you go?

Do you have any interesting family traditions?

Have you ever been seriously injured?

Has anyone ever broken your heart? Are you really over it?

What's your favorite form of communication?

What's the best way to spend your birthday?

Who do you think is the funniest person alive?

If you could be a character from a movie, who would you be?

What's the farthest you've ever travelled? Why did you go there?

Do you prefer a detailed plan, or going with the flow?

Have you ever won a medal? What was it for?

Have you ever been stuck in an elevator? Who were you with and how did you cope?

Did you like going to school? Would you like to do it all over again?

What's the best way to help and encourage someone to learn something?

Who do you think is the funniest person alive?

If you could travel in time, what era would you visit?

What is guaranteed to put a smile on your face?

What was the last song that you just couldn't get out of your head?

What would you say to an alien visitor to earth?

Have you ever had an imaginary friend? What were they like?

If you could have one wish granted, what would it be?

Do you have any bad habits? What are they?

What do you hope to achieve in your life?

What are the best and worst things about your life?

What's the most stupid thing you've ever done?

Do you prefer city life or the countryside?

If you could only ever wear one outfit, what would it be?

If you had an extra hour in the day,
how would you use it?

Do you make New Year's resolutions
and if so, do you keep them?

What's the best view you've ever seen?

Do you prefer to follow the lead of
others, or be the leader?

Why do you think some people do bad things?

What in the world do you think is beautiful?

Have you ever kept a secret or do you
always tell someone eventually?

Do you prefer life to be easy or to be
challenging? Why do you think this is?

What fact about you would surprise me?

24

Diane Weston

Are you bright and breezy in the morning, or bleary eyed and grumpy?

What's your favorite time of the year?

What's your favorite way to get some exercise?

Do you collect anything? If so, what is it?

What type of scenery would you most prefer to be the view from your house?

Do you like to take vacations close to home or in far flung destinations?

How well do you think you'd cope with being famous and having your private life talked about in the press?

What is your favorite childhood memory?

What fact about you would surprise me?

What is most likely to make you feel sentimental?

What 3 items would you take to a desert island?

What is your favorite type of weather?

What song is most likely to get you up on the dancefloor?

What place would you never want to visit again?

You've got 20 dollars to spend right now, what are you buying?

What were your best and worst subjects at school?

What would you say you're best at?

How would other people describe you?

If you could know the answer to one question, what would you ask?

What are the highest and lowest points of your life so far?

What's the best meal out you've ever had?

Do you prefer to read books or watch movies?

Do you love getting gifts or would you really prefer money?

What websites do you visit most often?

What movie, TV series and book would you tell everyone to avoid?

Have you ever had a vacation that's gone wrong? What happened?

What's the best way to help people?

What is your worst nightmare?

What's the toughest thing you've ever had to do?

Are you happy with yourself or are you always trying to change?

What's the most fun you ever had?

What's the weirdest gift you've ever received?

If you could invent something, what would it be?

Do you like to have the latest technology or do you prefer others to try things first?

What items do you always carry around with you?

What do you think makes different people like different things?

Have you ever had an emergency plane landing? Did it put you off flying?

What's the best advice you've ever been given?

What is your biggest problem and do you think you'll overcome it?

What frustrates you the most?

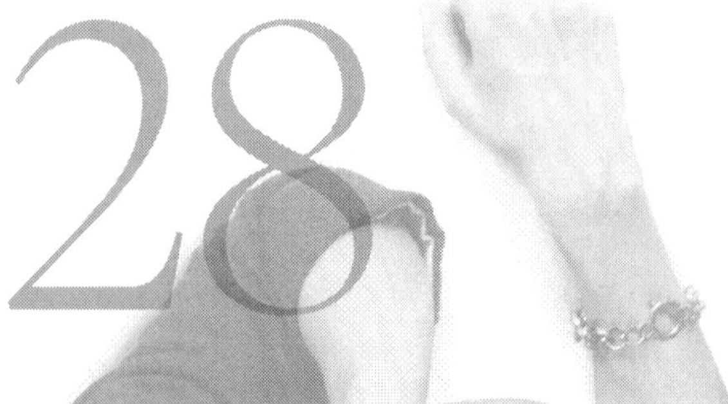

If you could invent something, what would it be?

Do you have any tattoos? If so, what do they mean to you?

What's the most you've ever spent on an item of clothing? Was it worth it?

If you were in a rock band, what would your band be called?

What's your biggest fashion mistake?

If you could suddenly have a talent, what would it be?

Have you ever been mistaken for anyone else? Did you correct them?

What is it that makes you different from everyone else?

If you're feeling down, do you prefer being around people or being alone?

What's the worst behaviour you've ever witnessed?

What do you do that helps other people?

What are your major hobbies?

What's the most pointless trend you've ever joined in with?

Which room in your house is your favorite and why?

If the world was going to end in 10 minutes, what would you do?

Do you believe in any conspiracy theories? If so, what are they?

What is your earliest memory?

What's the worst insult you've ever had?

Have you ever stolen anything? If so, what was it?

In what ways have you changed over the last 10 years?

Do you think there are ever any benefits to having an argument?

On a night out, what drink are you most likely to order?

What's the last thing you learned to do?

What do you want to do when you retire?

If you had to live in another country
for a year, where would you go?

What do you least like spending your money on?

Has anyone ever copied your style,
why do you think they did that?

What are three interesting things about yourself?

What really gives you the creeps?

Who is the most interesting or unusual
member of your family and why?

Do you think people can ever change
their true personalities?

What really gives you the creeps?

What subject would you be best at teaching?

Which sport do you find the most exciting,
and which the most boring?

What is your most treasured possession?

Do you play videogames? If so, which do you like best?

What are the best and worst things
about living in your country?

Do you think there should be extra
taxes on unhealthy foods?

If you could go on a date with anyone, who would it be?

What's the best way to make friends with someone?

What's the nicest thing anyone has ever done for you?

What's the worst thing you've ever said to someone?

Diane Weston

If you could have any animal as a pet, what would you choose?

What language would you most like to be fluent in?

Did you go to school with anyone who became really successful?

What's the best movie you've seen this year?

What do you do sometimes, that you'd like to do more often?

How many times have you moved house? Why did you move?

If you went back in time, how could you most impress the people of the past?

Have you ever taught yourself to do something? What was it?

Do you believe in an afterlife or reincarnation?

What advice would you give your teenage self?

Which member of your family is most like you?

36

Diane Weston

What's the best thing you've ever been given for free?

Do you have any lucky charms or rituals?

If you could be best friends with a cartoon character, who would you choose?

Do you like to visit popular places, or discover places other people don't often visit?

What's your best chat up line?

What are your guilty pleasures?

Who has had the greatest influence on your life?

Which member of your family is most like you?

Have you ever said something then instantly regretted it? What did you say?

Have you ever chosen to end a friendship? Why did you do this?

Whose sense of style do you most admire?

If you were a storybook villain,
what would be your name?

If you could only eat one meal for the rest of your life, what would you choose?

If you could move to a fictional world, from a book or from the screen, where would you live?

What's the best prank you've ever witnessed or taken part in?

Do you have any superstitions? What are they?

What do you feel is worse, someone who doesn't reply to your messages or someone who sends loads of messages all the time?

How much of our personalities do you think we're born with, and how much is down to the lives we live and how we're raised?

How do you know when you love someone?

Have you ever discovered something that truly shocked you?

What's the strangest thing you've got lurking in your fridge?

Have you ever been known by a nickname? How did it come about?

Have you ever hand made anything? What was it?

How many countries have you visited and which was your favorite?

Which sports person do you most admire?

Have you ever done a dare? What did you do?

Is there anything that gets on your nerves but doesn't seem to annoy anyone else?

Do you think having to overcome many obstacles makes someone a better person?

How do you think the world has changed since your childhood?

Have you ever really hated anyone?

If you could only ever read one book what would it be?

What's the best dream you've ever had?

Other than clothing, what 3 items would you pack for a vacation?

Are you good at creating a balance between work and fun times?

What do you think is most influential, the spoken word, the written word or film?

Do you think you're mostly a positive or a negative person? Would you prefer it to be different?

What about a person makes them beautiful in your eyes?

How important is it for you to be in a relationship?

Has anyone ever saved your life? What happened?

What's the greatest risk you've ever taken in life?

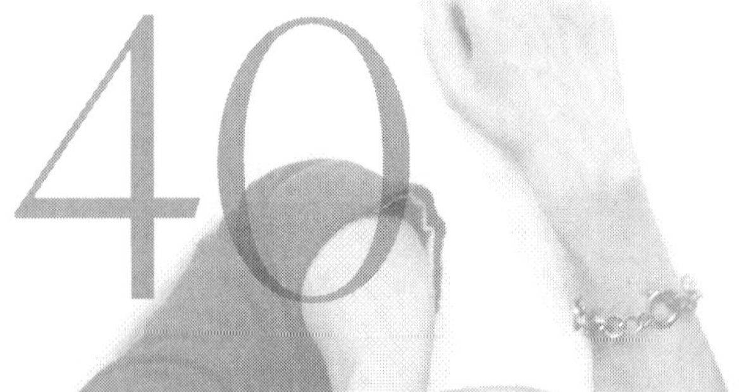

Has anyone ever saved your life? What happened?

If you had one minute to be on TV with the whole world watching, what would you say?

What do you think will be invented in the next twenty years?

If you got the chance to go to another planet but knew you couldn't come back, would you go?

You've written your autobiography, what is its title?

Have you ever complained in a restaurant? What happened?

Are you good in a crisis or do you panic?

Have you ever been envious of someone? Why?

Where in the world do you feel the safest?

If you could only leave one piece of advice for your descendants, what would it be?

When was the last time you were angry? How did you react?

42

Diane Weston

If you could be an animal, what would you choose to be and why?

What's the funniest joke you know?

If you could marry a celebrity, who would it be?

Have you ever drastically changed your appearance? What did you do?

You can have one super power – what is it?

What would you like to be remembered for?

Have you ever felt like your life was in danger?

What's the worst piece of advice you've ever been given?

Has helping someone ever backfired on you?

Have you ever been a victim of a house invasion? How did it make you feel?

What are 3 things you'd like to do before you die?

44

Diane Weston

What photo did you last take on your phone?

What is your favorite holiday and why is it so special to you?

Is there a word you always struggle to pronounce? What is it?

What did you believe as a kid but then found out to be untrue?

What in your opinion would be the worst name you could have been given?

What are 3 things you'd like to do before you die?

Have you ever stepped in to help a stranger?

At what age did you feel the happiest?

Have you ever posted something on social media and regretted it?

What issue do you feel most strongly about?

What's the best Halloween costume you've ever worn?

Have you ever got rid of something and really regretted it? What was it?

Do you have any plans for next year?

Have you ever followed a diet? Did it work?

What's your go-to user name and where did it come from?

What would make you the happiest?

How would you like your partner to describe you?

How do you hope your life will be in 10 years time?

Have your first impressions of someone ever been totally wrong?

Has your relationship with your partner changed over time? In what way?

Do you enjoy extreme sports? Which ones?

Do you like to eat from a buffet or do you prefer to order from a menu?

If you could banish one species of animal or insect from the world, what would it be?

What do you think is the best thing that has been invented in the last 50 years?

Is there an activity you used to enjoy but don't care for anymore?

Do you think that workplace gossip and bullying is as much of a problem as it is in the schoolyard?

What is the most rewarding part of your life?

What did your parents do that really made you respect them?

Would you be able to have a relationship with someone if you didn't speak the same language?

What's the scariest thing anyone has ever said to you?

Do you like hustle and bustle or peace and quiet?

Do you ever research people you used to know on social media?

If you could do any job for a week, what job would you like to do?

If you were a convicted felon, what would you order for your last meal?

What do you think will be the next big invention that everyone will want to have?

Who do you think has made the world a better place?

Do you have any religious or spiritual beliefs? What are they?

Are you similar to your siblings or totally different?

What inventions do you think have made the world worse?

What is your most memorable failure?

What is your most memorable failure?

Is there any food you've never tried but really want to?

What has been your biggest impulse buy?

If you were invited to go on a TV reality show, would you do it?

Would you be good on a TV quiz show?

Do you keep a diary? Would you let anyone else read it?

Do you think the world would be a better place without social media?

If there was a tracker on your phone, would your loved ones be surprised about where you go?

Do you think technology is making education better, or distracting from learning?

Would you be embarrassed if your Internet search history was published for all to see?

What's the biggest lie you've ever told?

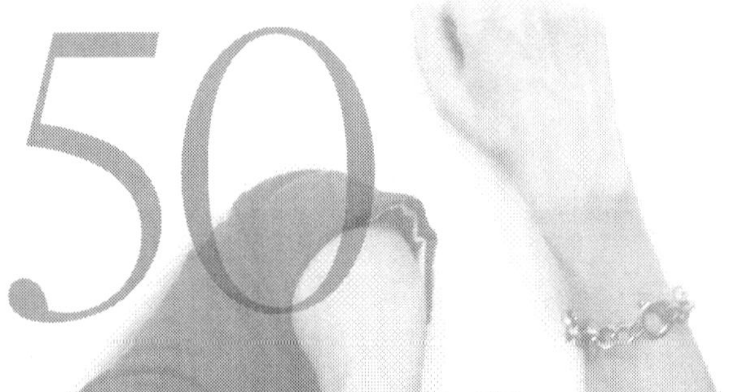

Would you move to another country on the other side of the world for someone you loved?

Do you tend to learn from your mistakes, or make the same mistake over and over again?

How do you think your classmates remember you?

What's the biggest favor you've ever done someone?

What's the most important item you've ever lost? Did you get it back?

If your house was on fire, what would you try to save first?

What mistakes did your parents make that you'll be careful to avoid?

Do you think Covid-19 has changed the world forever? In what way?

Has anything ever made you run away screaming? What was it?

What is the biggest argument you've ever had with someone? Did you ever make up?

What subject would you study if you went back to school for a year?

What is your biggest extravagance?

If there was a movie about your life, who would you like to play the part of you?

What would be your perfect hairstyle?

What do you miss about being a child?

Have you ever seen something in another country that totally confused you?

What is something you wish you'd done when you were younger but never did?

What's the best thing about being a grown up?

Under what circumstances would you say it's okay to check someone else's phone messages?

What in life do you really dread?

Have you ever performed a random act of kindness? What did you do?

What do you prefer? A long telephone conversation, or exchanging text messages?

What's your favorite type of food?

What would be your perfect road trip adventure? Where would you go and who with?

If you found a wad of cash on the ground and no one was around, would you hand it in to the police or keep it?

What's the nicest compliment you've ever been given?

Have you ever heard a rumour about yourself that was totally wrong?

What made you realise that your parents didn't know the answer to every question you asked?

What's the wildest thing you've ever done?

Do you feel guilty about anything from your past?

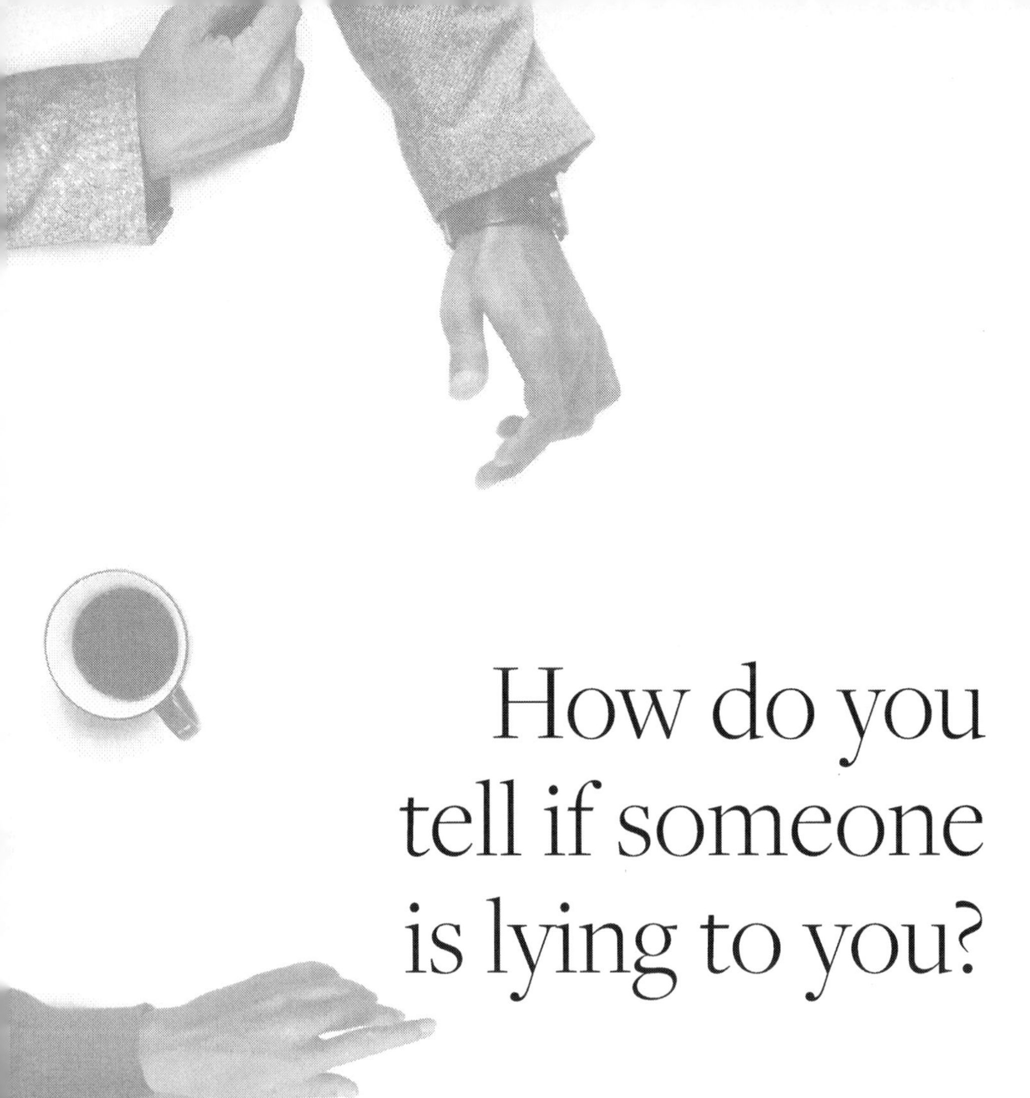

How do you tell if someone is lying to you?

54

Diane Weston

Would you like to be a member of a royal family? Why?

Have you ever seen a ghost?

What's the worst thing a guest has ever done in your home?

What's the best gift you've ever given someone?

Would you be happy to wear clothes someone else had chosen for you?

What would you rather be doing right now?

What would your idea of hell be? How about your perfect heaven?

Have you had a role model in life? Who is it?

How do you tell if someone is lying to you?

Have you ever been falsely accused of something? Did you manage to prove your innocence?

What item in your kitchen could you not live without?

If it was one season all year round, what season would you choose and why?

What's the weirdest wrong number call or message you've ever received?

If someone has a different opinion to you, do you try to change their mind or agree to disagree?

What's the best way to surprise someone?

Have you ever forgotten to do something really important? What were the consequences?

Has a stranger ever made a huge impact on you? Why?

Have you ever lost contact with someone and wish you could meet up with them again?

Do you do anything that could be considered as politically incorrect? What is it?

Have you ever caught someone out who was lying?

If music played wherever you walked,
what would your theme tune be?

Would you have a chip implanted in your body
that would make payments and open doors?

What do you do that most annoys other people?

What do other people like to talk about
that you find really boring?

Is there anything you'd like to do but are too scared to?

Is there anything you do or own that others
would call childish but you just don't care?

Would your 12 year old self be happy
with how your life has turned out?

What worries you more, the past catching up
with you, or the unknown of the future?

Did you do anything as a kid that is still
talked about in your family to this day?

Do you know something that could ruin
someone's life if it ever got out?

Who do you think is the most overrated celebrity?

A genie grants you 3 wishes – what are they?

If you had to have a catchphrase, what would it be?

What's the worst excuse you've ever made to get out of doing something?

What food do you hate the look of but love the taste of?

Do you have a memory that makes you smile every time you think of it?

Do you think you'd be able to effectively homeschool a child? What would be your best subject to teach?

Do you think most people put on a front and deep down they are quite different?

Have you ever cheated in a relationship or been cheated on?

Have you ever been in a court room? How did this come about?

A genie grants you 3 wishes – what are they?

Do you sleepwalk or talk in your sleep?
Has it ever caused you trouble?

Is there something that you love, but most people hate?

What's the best thing to do in your town?

Have you ever broken something while browsing in a store? Did you have to pay for it?

What's the strangest thing you've ever seen on social media?

Do you think plastic surgery generally makes people look better or worse?

Have you ever worn an outfit that was totally inappropriate for the event?

What is the worst insult you've ever received?

Have you ever been afraid of someone? Why?

In what circumstances do you feel out of your comfort zone?

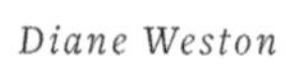

What's the worst chat up line you've ever heard?

What language do you think sounds the nicest?

What is your signature dish?

What's the worst vacation you've ever been on?

What's the worst job you've ever had?

What do you think are the benefits of spending time in many different countries?

What habits would totally put you off a person?

Do you think your education was actually valuable to you in life?

What would you do if you thought someone was being abused?

What are your greatest worries for future generations?

What would you say takes up most of your time?

62

Diane Weston

What type of theme park ride would you go on again and again?

Do you think it would be better to be famous, or very rich?

What would you say takes up most of your time?

Do you like to be fashionable, or create your own unique style?

What's the strangest story you've seen on the news?

Do you think highly intelligent people have less common sense?

What's the worst thing about meeting someone for the first time?

Have you ever fallen in love with someone you hadn't met in real life?

Has a guest ever overstayed their welcome? How did you get rid of them?

Have you ever been to a wedding and thought it wouldn't last? Were you right?

What is your favorite simple pleasure?

Are you currently learning to do anything
or improving a skill you already have?

Have you ever got lost? Where were you?

Are you trying to quit any habits?

Who was your favorite teacher at school and
what made them stand out from the rest?

Do you believe in extra-terrestrial life?

What tip or hack have you learnt that
really made your life easier?

Is there anything about you that your
best friend doesn't know?

Would you marry someone if you had any doubts at all?

Is there anything you regret telling someone?

Would you rather have the car of your dreams or the house of your dreams?

Have you ever ordered a dish on a menu only to find it wasn't at all what you imagined?

What is the most interesting, but pointless fact you know?

Do you like your name? Do you think it suits you?

What's the most expensive thing you've ever broken?

Have you ever argued with someone on the Internet? What was it about?

Have you ever burst out laughing in a totally inappropriate situation?

Have you ever taken revenge on someone? What did you do?

What would you like your last words to be?

Do you think it's worse to regret something you did, or something you didn't do?

Which restaurant dish do you wish you could perfectly recreate at home?

What place or event were you really looking forward to going to but found disappointing?

In your opinion, what are the best toppings for a pizza?

If you could invent a new subject to be taught in schools, what would it be?

If you could remove one task from your daily routine, what would it be?

How much do you think your life differs to that of your parents when they were your age?

What have you seen and wished you hadn't?

How do you feel when you look back at old photos of yourself?

Have you ever lost your respect for someone? How did that come about?

What's the most disrespectful behavior you ever witnessed?

What have you seen and wished you hadn't?

What do you think is your best personality trait?

Have you ever raised money for charity? What did you do?

Have you ever slept through your alarm? Did it ruin your plans?

Do you think sci-fi movies and books influence the future as inventors use them for inspiration?

Have you ever eaten a meal in a restaurant then realised you have no way to pay? What happened?

How do you think the world would work if everyone looked the same?

Have you ever been picked on for the way you looked? How did it make you feel?

Have you ever visited a therapist? Do you think it helped you?

Do you believe that most people are good and honest?

What do you think is the hardest thing about being a child?

What item were you really excited to own that didn't live up to your expectations?

What was the most pointless subject you studied at school?

Do people think you're older or younger than you actually are?

Do you ever have the same dream repeatedly? What is it about?

You can have one wish granted, and the same wish is also granted for everyone else in the world. What do you wish for?

What product would you like to have invented?

Has anyone ever asked you to change something about yourself? Did you do it?

Have you ever told a lie to impress someone? Did they ever find out the truth?

If you knew a good friend had committed a crime, would you report them?

What are other people embarrassed about that you're totally fine with?

What is the coolest place you've ever been to?

What is the most annoying thing about your daily life?

If you could invent a word, what would it be and what would it mean?

What are you interested in that would surprise most people?

Have you ever travelled for work? Where have you been?

What's your favorite takeout order?

Do you think self-driving cars are a great idea or a dangerous invention?

Have you ever overheard a conversation and discovered something you shouldn't have?

What is the most heart warming story you have ever heard?

Have you ever been ripped off? What happened?

If you had to put on a five minute show, what would you do?

How many places have you lived in? Which was your favorite?

Do you think you could live in a cave in the wild for a month? Would it have any benefits?

What's the best surprise you've ever had?

Do you think modern technology saves time or makes life more complicated?

Would you like to run your own business? What type of business would it be?

Have you ever been to a party that went horribly wrong? What happened?

How have your kids embarrassed you, or how did you embarrass your parents as a child?

Do you think you've ever been influenced by an influencer?

What's your most memorable 'life isn't fair' moment?

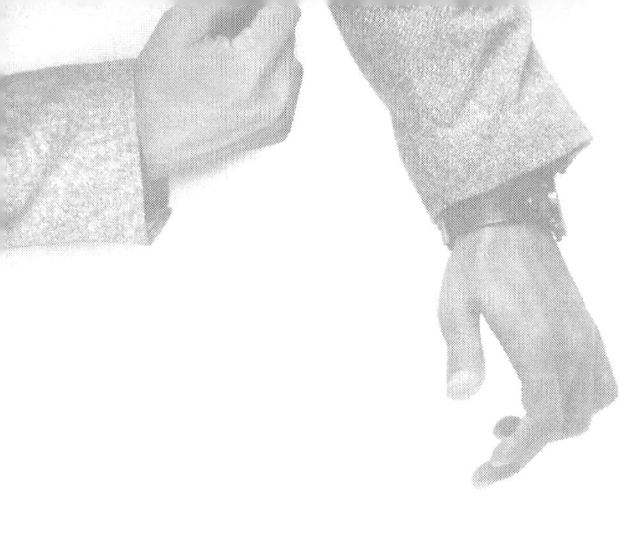

How do you think the world will end?

72

Diane Weston

If you had paints and a canvas right now, what would you paint?

What is your favorite soundtrack?

What's your favorite place to go for a walk?

What app did you think would be really good but you never use it?

What is popular now that you predict will seem stupid in five years time?

Have you ever had to hold your tongue when really you wanted to say something?

In what ways do you think the world has changed over the last decade?

Do you think the world is more dangerous now than a generation ago?

Do you believe that some people are born lucky?

How do you think the world will end?

You've just won the lottery, what is the first thing you do?

What would you say is the best way to stay healthy?

Would you rather work for everything you have at a job you love, or be given everything you want?

When you feel really stressed or angry, what do you do to calm yourself down?

Do you trust anyone enough to give them your bank card number or tell them your passwords?

What's the longest you've gone without sleeping and why?

Do you think good looks or intelligence will get you further in life?

If you could relive a year of your life, which year would you pick and why?

What do you think love is?

Diane Weston

What's the weirdest thing you've ever eaten?

What are you most looking forward to?

You can take one person on a 5 star holiday for a week, who are you taking?

Do you like foreign films? Do you prefer them dubbed or with subtitles?

Have you ever had a secret admirer? Did you find out who it was?

What's the most daring thing you have ever done?

Has anyone ever managed to totally change your opinion?

What have you done that you would never want to do again?

If you could bring one person back from the dead, who would it be?

What is something that has got you in trouble?

What recipe always reminds you of home?

If your family had a motto, what would it be?

Do you have any famous relations? If not, who would you like to be related to?

What are you most grateful for?

If you had to trade places with a member of your family, who would it be?

If you framed a quote for your wall, what would it say?

Do you tend to trust your heart or your head the most?

Has anyone ever played a practical joke on you? What was it?

How do you think the world might work if there were no money?

Do you think you'd be able to maintain a long distance relationship?

Have you ever fallen asleep somewhere you shouldn't have? Where?

What's the most hilarious thing a kid has ever said to you?

If you started a club, what would it be for?

If you could ask a famous person one question and they had to answer truthfully, who would you ask and what would you ask them?

What TV family is most like your own?

Have you ever missed an important train or flight? Did it work out alright in the end?

Have you ever shared a room or a house with someone really odd?

If you could find out the date and time of your death, would you want to know?

What do you wish you had more time for?

What's the most awkward situation you've ever found yourself in?

What's the best way to cope with the ending of a relationship?

78

Diane Weston

You're having a dinner party and can invite 4 people, from the present or the past. Who are you inviting?

What item do you think would seem most magical if you took it back to medieval times?

What rules did you have growing up that you thought were stupid?

Are there any other names that your parents nearly called you, or would have called you if you were the opposite sex?

Is there anyone you know that you would like to know much better?

Do your likes and dislikes change often, or do you tend to keep liking the same things?

If you had to lose one of your senses, which would it be and why?

To what degree do you think your parents have influenced your life?

What's the best way to cope with the ending of a relationship?

What do think makes some people popular and others less so?

If someone gave you something really valuable to look after, where would you hide it?

What do you think was the most important event in the history of mankind?

Do you like to stay up late or get an early night?

What's the best bargain you've ever bought second hand?

What event in your life were you dreading but ended up enjoying yourself?

Do you think the news reports we read and see on TV are accurate?

Who has upset you the most in your life?

What's the worst place you've ever spent the night?

If you were to propose to someone, how would you do it?

When do you most feel like the true, real you?

If you opened a restaurant, what would it be called?

Do you think space tourism will become popular in the future?

What are your best and worst vegetables to eat?

What are the best and worst jobs you've ever had?

Can you describe your ideal partner?

Which of your friends is least like yourself and why do you get along?

Do you have any controversial opinions? What are they?

When was someone last kind to you? What did they do?

Do you think it's harder to be a kid these days?

Have you ever felt obsessed with someone or something?

Do you have a side line alongside your regular job? What is it?

Do you think people have an online persona and a real persona and they're very different?

Do you feel like life is a rollercoaster?

Do you think sports people deserve the high wages they're paid?

What could you do to be a better person?

What's the worst punishment you've ever been given?

What could your partner do that you'd never forgive them for?

What situations make you feel most uncomfortable?

Do you find it hard to say no when someone asks you for a favour?

On the whole, do you think you've been treated fairly in life?

What's the worst punishment you've ever been given?

Do you think celebrities that advertise products really use those products?

What's the most disappointing movie you've ever seen?

Do you think what your wear influences how you feel?

What's the first thing you tend to notice about people?

What's the strangest food combination you've ever eaten? Was it good?

What do you think are the best and worst jobs in the world?

If you were in big trouble, who would you call?

If you knew a friend's partner was cheating on them, would you tell them?

What do you think are the most common reasons for relationships ending?

What situations make you feel unsafe?

What is popular at the moment that you really don't like?

You have some free time, do you spend it being active, or relaxing?

If you had a YouTube channel, what would it be about?

What does the word 'home' mean to you?

What is the worst part of the day?

If you were reincarnated, what would you like to come back as?

Do you think that men and women really can be just good friends?

Do you believe some people are destined to be together?

Who is the most successful person you know? Are they happy?

Can money buy you happiness?

Do you do any volunteering?

What's the most embarrassing song you know all the words to?

What food would you find hardest to give up?

Would you ever want to move back in with your parents? If you live with your parents, do you want to move out?

What bad habits did you used to have but gave up?

What has been the biggest waste of time in your life so far?

What's your best advice for someone starting out doing the same job as you?

What's the best way to discover something new?

Do you let your emotions get the better of you? Which emotion is hardest to deal with?

When did you last feel jealous?

Who was your best friend in school?
Are you still friends now?

Which country do you think offers
the best standard of living?

What would you do if someone left
a baby on your doorstep?

Who are the happiest couple you know and
why do you think they're so happy?

Are there any song lyrics that really
mean a lot to you? What are they?

Why do you think that some people
have amazing talents?

What are you fed up of explaining to people?

Have you ever thrown someone
out of your house? Why?

What's the meanest thing anyone has ever said to you?

If you received a note that said 'I know what
you did' what would you think they meant?

What is your favorite memory of your grandparents?

88

Diane Weston

What's the best or most unusual lost item you've found? Did you keep it or find its owner?

Is there anything that isn't illegal, but you think it should be?

What is your favorite memory of your grandparents?

Do you think you would make a good politician? Why?

Have you ever been thrown out of a bar or restaurant? Why?

Have you ever tried to communicate something telepathically? Do you think it worked?

Have you ever been in a physical fight? What caused it?

Were you ever given detention at school? What was it for?

Do you think you can spend time with a small child and know what they'll be like when they grow up?

What's the most unreasonable thing anyone has ever asked of you?

What's the oddest name you've ever heard? Was it someone you knew?

Have you ever been on a sports team? Was your team successful?

Would you be good in an eating contest? What food would you choose?

Have you ever had an operation? What was it for?

Have you ever dated someone with a big age gap? Did the difference matter to you?

Imagine you have two children and you can choose their professions – what you want them to be?

Is there anything you've done, good or bad, that no one else knows about but you?

Do you do anything that other people think is weird?

Have you ever learnt something about a friend or family member that truly shocked you?

How old do you think someone needs to be, to truly be an adult?

Diane Weston

Do you ever worry about monsters in the night, even though you know they're not really there?

What food tastes as good cold the next day as when it was hot and freshly cooked?

What have you had to explain to someone that you thought everyone knew?

If you designed a t-shirt to wear every day, what design would you have?

If you could get rid of one person from the world, who would it be?

Have you ever faked being sick? What were you trying to avoid?

Is there anything you're scared of that didn't bother you as a child?

What one thing have you learnt in life that you wish you'd known earlier?

How would you feel if your parents split up? If this has happened, how did it make you feel?

Have you ever had a bad vibe from a person or a place that you just couldn't explain?

Can you control what happens in your dreams?

Have you ever believed an urban myth? What was it?

Do you like to follow a recipe or make up your own unique dishes?

Do you think it's true that healthy eating costs more than eating junk food?

Who is the most embarrassing person to be around and why?

Have you ever tried online dating? How did it work out for you?

What is the saddest story you've ever heard?

Has anything ever happened in your life that you will never fully get over?

Have you ever trusted your gut on something and it worked out to be for the best?

Have you ever badly let someone down? Did they forgive you?

Where do you think all the lost socks go?

Who is the most eccentric person you know?

Do you have pets with any special talents?

Have you ever been fired from a job?
Was your next job better?

Which celebrity would you like to have gone to school with?

You get an all expenses paid trip to anywhere in the world but you have to go alone – where do you go?

Have you ever done a social media challenge? What was it?

What is something that your true friends can say to you but other people can't?

What did your parents get wrong while raising you?

Have you ever made someone cry? What did you do?

What word do you have an irrational hatred of?

94

Diane Weston

What has been the highlight of your week?

If you could invent a cocktail, what would be in it and what would you call it?

What is your favorite number and what is the reason you like that number best?

What word do you have an irrational hatred of?

What was the last thing you bought a ticket for? Was it worth it?

If you could start your life over again, would you do it?

What's the most spontaneous thing you've ever done?

What's the most disgusting thing you've ever had to do?

Where and with whom do you truly feel you belong?

What makes you feel vulnerable?

Have you ever performed on stage? What did you do?

What's the geekiest thing you do in your spare time?

If you could win an award, what would you like it to be for?

What color would say best represents you? Is this your favorite color?

If you wanted to take over the earth, what would be your plan?

Do you think that most people who get tattoos regret them?

Do you feel like time goes too fast or too slow, or does it differ depending on what you're doing?

What was the last thing that made you laugh out loud?

What is the worst piece of advice you've ever given someone?

Do you think every human being has a purpose in life?

What chore are you most likely to put off doing?

If something good happens, who is the first person you tell?

Do you think you look like your pet? Do you know anyone who looks like their pet?

Do you have an item of clothing that's worn out but you just can't throw it away?

Did you have any obsessions as a kid? Are you still into them?

If you could teleport to anywhere on earth for one hour, where would you go?

How old do you feel on the inside?

Do you like the way you look?

What do you think makes humans different from other animals?

What do you miss most about your partner when you're not together?

What is your most useful possession?

What's your favorite reason to celebrate?

Do you know your neighbours well? Do you like them?

Are you good at saving? What are you saving for?

Would you like to have more free time?
What would you do with it?

Could you date someone with very different political or religious views to you?

Which emotion do you consider to be the least attractive?

Do you think relationships are better when you start out as friends?

Do you think it's ever right to lie or withhold the truth?

What does marriage mean to you?

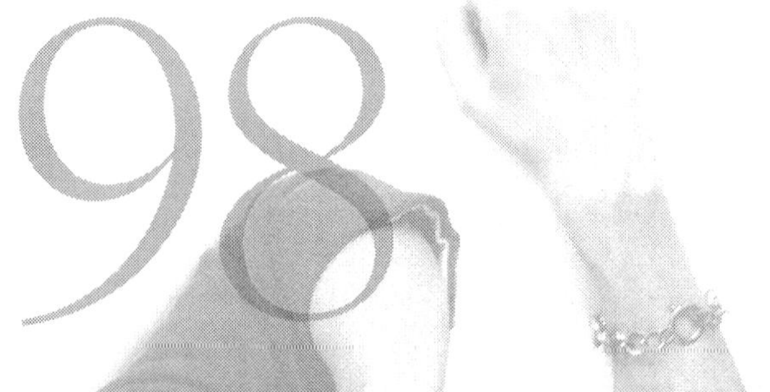

Who do you think is the most
attractive person on the planet?

Where is the best place to go on honeymoon?

What's the luckiest thing that has ever happened to you?

What is your best quality?

Who do think would be most upset if you died?

What is your greatest weakness?

Do you think partners should share
all the chores equally?

How do you feel when you fail at something?

Why did your last relationship end?
Do you wish it hadn't?

Is there anyone who you wish you'd never met?

At what moment did you feel most loved?

100

Diane Weston

Who in your life are you most honest with?

Are you a person who likes hugs and displays of affection?

Do you think you're attractive?

Do you think you could be happy in the same relationship for 50 years?

Are you more likely to live in the moment or plan for the future?

Do you think that most people know the real you?

Are you easily convinced to do something you don't want to do? Do you think it's good to try new things?

At what moment did you feel most loved?

How do you think your life would change if you were in a wheelchair?

Has there ever been a time in your life when you've felt truly alone?

At what time of day are you the most productive?

How do you like your eggs in the morning?

Are you generally outgoing or more reserved?

What 3 qualities do you value most in a person?

Do you think everyone should have children?

Do you think anyone can turn their life around if they try hard enough?

Have you ever broken anything out of anger? Did you regret it?

Do you believe in giving people a second chance?

What's the biggest compromise you've ever had to make?

Have you ever learnt a lesson the hard way? What happened?

If you woke up tomorrow and everyone had disappeared, what would you do?

How do you think humans will evolve over the next 10,000 years?

What's your best money saving tip?

Have you ever pretended to like someone? Why?

Do you think children are more badly behaved now than when you were young?

What is the worst illness you've ever had?

Has there ever been a feud in your family. Was it ever resolved?

Have you ever had to lie for someone? How did it make you feel?

Have you ever said 'I told you so' to someone? Why?

If your partner went to prison for 20 years and you knew they were not guilty, would you wait for them?

Do you think criminals are punished severely enough?

If someone knocked on your door in the middle of the night, would you answer it? Why?

How well do you cope with change?

Have you ever claimed someone else's idea as your own?

What's your favorite way to treat yourself?

What did you think was normal when you were growing up that you now find strange?

Have you ever lost a large sum of money? How did it happen?

Who do you think you have helped most in life? Do you think they are grateful?

Do you feel there are any life experiences you have missed out on?

Have you ever asked someone on a date and been turned down? How did it make you feel?

Have you ever claimed someone else's idea as your own?

Someone texts you at 3am, who is it most likely to be?

What other decade would you have liked to have been born in?

If you could haunt someone after your death, who would it be?

If you were unable to tell a lie for a week, do you think you would lose friends?

If you were leaving the planet forever but allowed to send all your contacts one final message, what would it say?

Do you think replacing human labor with robots is a good or bad idea?

Do you believe in astrology and do you think you're typical of your star sign?

Do you find it easy to admit when you're wrong? Why?

If your partner could read your mind, do you think they would stay with you?

What's a time when you've gone 'above and beyond' for someone?

What was the first film you ever saw at the cinema?

When you're grumpy, is it best to leave you alone or try to cheer you up?

What have you never done that you think you'd be terrible at?

If you could have free and painless plastic surgery, would you have it and what would you have done?

Do you feel your life is better now than it has ever been?

Do you think you've done more good or bad things in your life overall?

What age do you think is the best for starting a family?

When did someone last tell you that they loved you?

What do you envy most in other people?

Would you stay with a partner even if all your friends and family didn't like them?

What's your favorite daydream?

Do you believe in magic? Have you ever witnessed anything magical?

What's your favorite thing to do on a snowy day?

If your life was made into a movie, do you think it would be popular? Why?

What was the last new thing you tried?

Do you think the tough times in your life have made you stronger or weaker?

Do you feel your life has meaning? What is the meaning of your life?

Do you think the world would be any different if you hadn't been born? In what ways?

Which of the 7 deadly sins are you most guilty of and why?

Do you feel like your life is going in the right direction? What's next for you?

If you had to get rid of either tea, coffee, wine or beer, which one would you choose and why?

Was there a movie or TV show that particularly scared you as a child?

Do you think you work better alone or in as part of a team? Which do you actually prefer?

With money no object, what would be the most impressive way to spend a first date?

What is the top story people tell about you?

Have you ever ignored advice and regretted it later?

Is there anyone who would be glad if you moved far away?

Have you ever gone along with a crowd and done something you didn't really want to? What was it?

What did you do that made your parents the most upset?

Has anyone ever told you they are proud of you? What had you done?

What is the weirdest smell that you like?

110

Diane Weston

If everyone did what you told them, what's the first thing you'd say and who would you say it to?

What type of pet would you most like to own?

What is the weirdest smell that you like?

Do you prefer a simple or a complicated life? What do you have now?

Do you give up easily or do you keep trying until you succeed?

Would someone who last met you when you were ten recognise you today?

Do you feel you've missed out on opportunities? What do you think you've missed out on?

Would you be prepared to steal if you couldn't afford to feed your child?

Have you ever given up something you loved? What was it?

How does having kids change your life?

What do you think is really underrated and deserves to be more popular?

Do you think you'd do better if you redid your school years now?

What one thing do you hope is invented in your lifetime?

What do you like most and least about being in a relationship?

Is there something you find more difficult than other people? What is it?

Who do you think looks up to you?

When did something that happened by chance have a big impact on your life?

What do you wish you could say to someone but just can't?

Do you feel more positive or negative about the future? Why?

Do you feel that people underestimate you? Why do you think they do that?

Have you ever hugged or kissed someone by mistake? How did they react?

Have you ever been accidentally locked in somewhere? Where was it?

What's your all time favorite breakfast?

Are you a late person or an early person and have you ever tried to change this?

Have you ever apologised when you didn't mean it? What was it for?

Does pressure make you work harder, or hinder you?

What story about your childhood is most repeated by your parents?

What would instantly put you off someone who was otherwise very attractive?

How well do you think you would cope if you were sent to prison?

What truth has been the hardest to hear?

How important is money to you?

Have you ever met someone and felt like you've known them forever? Who was it?

Do you think the way you look matches your personality? If not, why?

If you had to take a vow of silence for a year, how well do you think you'd cope?

Would you rather do something well paid, or something you loved? Why?

Is there are question you're sick of being asked? What is it?

Are you generally trusting or more wary? Do you think this is for the best?

Have you ever not asked a question because you were afraid of the answer?

What are you most likely to get defensive about?

Has curiosity ever got you into trouble? What happened?

What are you most likely to get defensive about?

If you had to sing a song live on TV, what would you sing?

What do you secretly love but don't admit up to?

What small gestures do you most appreciate?

If you went back to the 1980s how well do you think you'd be able to cope and what would you miss?

Are there things about you that you don't tell your parents or your children?

Do you have any worries or fears about getting older?

Have you ever ended a relationship then regretted it when it was too late?

What's the worst time you let someone down?

Have you ever made an enemy?

What would someone envy about you?

Which famous person do you find the most irritating?

Do you think the best day of your life is yet to come?

Do you think that you mostly make the right decisions?

Have you ever broken any bones? How did it happen?

Who loves you most in the world?

What are you most self-conscious about?

What are two things you absolutely can't compromise on?

Do you think your partner would have liked you if they had met you ten years previously?

Is there anything you wish you'd done earlier or later in life than you did?

Have you ever told someone a secret and regretted it?

Is there something you find funny that your partner doesn't?

What did you used to think was cool that really wasn't?

What are your top 3 films for a movie marathon?

What did your parents tell you not to do that you did anyway?

Do you believe that everything happens for a reason?

Do you think people change a lot or generally stay the same?

When it comes to relationships, do you have a 'type'? What is it?

Do you think your parents treated you and your siblings equally? If you're an only child, do you wish you had siblings?

What part of being an adult is harder than you thought it would be?

Who do you think will play the biggest roles in your life in 10 years time?

Which Disney prince or princess is most like you?

Is there anything you'd say you're an expert on?

Do you believe that opposites attract, or that being similar to someone is better?

What song would you like playing at your funeral?

What are your financial goals?

Is there something you say that actually annoys you when you say it?

Have you ever walked out on a job? What made you leave?

What do you think will be the biggest problems for the next generation?

What are 3 things you're thankful for?

Is there anyone you trust 100%?

Can you sum up your life so far in four sentences?

120

Diane Weston

What subjects would you like to know more about and become an expert on?

How do you show people that you care?

What thoughts go through your head when you can't sleep?

In what ways are you artistic or creative?

Who was your first ever friend? Are you still in touch with them?

Can you sum up your life so far in four sentences?

What's the best way to make up with someone after a fall out?

Do you ever feel very sad or very happy for no reason? Why do you think this is?

How did your parents meet each other?

If you could ask God one questions, what would it be?

Have you ever visited a fortune teller or psychic? Did what they tell you come true?

If you could advertise a product, what would it be?

Do you think you'd get on with your own clone?

Is there a story behind your name?
Why did your parents choose it?

If you want to go out and have a good time, who do you call and why?

What emojis do you use the most?

Would you consider yourself to be a good friend? Why?

If this week started over, what would you change about it?

Are your good memories or bad ones the most vivid?

What do you think holds you back most in life?

When did you last write a letter and who did you send it to?

When and where did you first go on vacation without your parents?

What music genre would people be surprised that you like?

Has anyone ever made something for you? What was it?

If you went into space and met someone from another planet, how would you describe earth?

How did you meet your best friend?

Have you ever had a pen pal? Where did they live?

Do you think that only humans can really experience love?

Do you think our souls persist when our bodies are gone?

Do you think people should have a right to end their own lives? In what circumstances?

What are your top 3 video games of all time?

What has been your biggest cooking disaster?

What's the most extreme weather you've ever been out in?

At what age do you think people are generally happiest?

What cars would you most and least like to drive?

Do you think most celebrities deserve their fame and fortune?

Why do you think it is that we all have different likes and dislikes?

Where do you go when you want to be alone?

Do you think you're happier now than when you were a child?

What current world issues do you think are most important?

Where do you go when you want to be alone?

What's the best thing to do on your birthday?

What would be the worst and best colors to paint your entire house?

If you could instantly be able to play an instrument, what instrument would you choose?

Do you have any dietary restrictions? Are these by choice or for medical reasons?

What artwork is on your walls? Did you choose it?

Are there any charities that you feel are not worth supporting?

What do think is the most important language to be able to speak?

Do you think you appreciate things more if you've had to save up for them for a long time?

What physical traits run in your family?

How do you feel when friends do something without you?

Can you recommend any good podcasts?

Do you prefer dogs or cats? Why?

Have you always done the same job or have you changed career?

Would you rather have one large gift or 20 small ones? Why?

Do you eat to live or live to eat? Have you always been this way?

When have you felt completely immersed in another world? Was it a movie, a video game or something else?

Do you think a person's personality influences how physically attractive they appear to you?

If you were involved in politics, what would be your policies?

What's the best way to make someone do what you want?

What was an occasion when you felt you let yourself down?

If money were no object, what would you give your partner for their next birthday present?

What's the best April Fool's joke you've ever seen?

What's the funniest meme you've seen lately?

What is the best comeback you've ever given?

What do you think is the most over-hyped thing ever?

Do you ever skip meals? Which meal are you most likely to skip and why?

Would you consider yourself to be a romantic person? Why?

Have you ever walked out of a store and forgotten to pay? What happened?

What has made you feel ashamed of mankind?

Have you ever been the victim of a crime? What happened?

If you discovered a secret tunnel leading from your house, where would you like it to go?

What is your favorite TV commercial?

Do you know your IQ? If not, what would you guess it was?

What were you allowed to do as a child that you would never let your own kids do?

Which famous person from your country do you find most embarrassing?

If you could visit a huge museum all about a subject of your choosing, what would it be?

Do you find many people attractive or are you very selective?

Have you ever tried to put something right and made it worse? What happened?

Do you ever wish misfortune on anyone? Who and why?

What would you do if someone tried to blackmail you?

What's the worst case of bad manners you've ever witnessed?

130

Diane Weston

What item do people borrow from you that you wish they'd just go out and buy themselves?

Do you eat out of date food or get rid of it as soon as it expires?

What place in the world do you find the most boring?

If you knew you would go deaf in one hour, what would you like to listen to now?

Is there a photo of you that you wish you could completely erase from existence?

What's the worst case of bad manners you've ever witnessed?

What's the biggest coincidence that's ever happened in your life?

Have you ever been approached by a romance scammer? Did you fall for it?

What could someone say to you that would instantly make you angry?

Have you ever discovered a secret about someone after they passed away?

If you were dropped at the other side of your town, do you think you'd easily be able to find your way home on foot?

Would you be unhappy if all the photos on your phone were published online?

If all but one room in your house disappeared, which one would you keep?

What is a time when something has totally exceeded your expectations?

If the entire Internet was shut down today, what would you miss the most?

Have you ever pretended to be asleep? Why?

What's the weirdest meal someone has ever cooked for you? Did you eat it?

What excuse would you make if you really wanted to leave somewhere?

Has anyone ever called you a hero? What did you do to deserve it?

Was there ever a time when you knew something bad was happening and no one believed you?

Diane Weston

How easy do you think it would be to become homeless?

If someone from 3024 travelled back in time, what would you ask them?

What do you think you take most for granted in your life?

Have you ever helped a stranger in need? What did you do?

Who do you think has had the biggest negative effect on your life?

How do you think you will change over the next 20 years?

If there was a power cut this evening and you couldn't leave the house, what would you do?

Made in the USA
Monee, IL
28 November 2022